better together*

*This book is best read together, grownup and kid.

 akidsco.com

a kids
book
about

a kids book about body image

by Rebecca Alexander

a
kids
book
about

A Kids Book About books are available online: *akidsco.com*

To share your stories, ask questions, or inquire about bulk
purchases (schools, libraries, and nonprofits), please use
the following email address: *hello@akidsco.com*

ISBN: 978-1-951253-16-5

Designed and edited by Jelani Memory

For Bella and Baby M.

Intro

You were probably drawn to this book because you have a kid in your life. Period.

Not one single person is exempt from body image struggles. And yet, we rarely talk about these feelings with others. We feel alone in our insecurities. We feel like what's "wrong" with us is our fault.

We feel ashamed.

When we feel this way, very serious problems can arise. Eating disorders. Exercise disorders. Other forms of self-harm.

I hope this book will help you share the feelings you have about your body. I hope you'll talk about them. I hope you'll encourage your kids to do the same.

You might think you know
what this book is about,
but you really don't.

Yes, I'm going to talk about body image.

But you probably think that means I'm going to say things like...

You're beautiful just the way you are.

What you look like doesn't matter.

It's what's on the inside that counts.

If you love yourself, it shouldn't matter what other people think.

But...

this isn't a book about that.

You might believe all those things about other people, but you probably don't believe them about...

yourself.

You might hate the
way you sweat.

You might hate the way
you look in the mirror.

You might hate the
way your clothes fit.

You might hate the
size of your feet.

You might hate how
skinny your arms are.

You might hate
your body.

I've been there too.

And I still am sometimes.

You see, I'm big.

Like, really big.

I'm taller than average,

but what makes me
really big is...

I'm fat.

OK

OK

OK.

You might have heard
calling someone fat is mean.
That it's wrong.

And that definitely can be true.
Some people call other people fat
because they want to hurt
their feelings.

That is soooooooooooo not cool.
Don't do that.

But when I call myself fat,
I'm not being mean to myself.
I don't think being fat is a
bad thing anymore.

Being fat is just part of
who I am.

I'm also white.

I have blonde-ish hair
and green eyes.

I wear glasses and I walk
around with my dog a lot.

I'm usually smiling, but
sometimes I'm not.

I wear jeans.

I wear dresses.

I wear sneakers.

I wear high heels.

I wear bright colors.

I wear lots of black.

But...

when people see me on the
street, the first thing
they notice about
me is how
fat I am.

I wish they noticed
my cute outfits or
my friendly smile,
but they don't.

And sometimes
when I notice them
noticing how fat I am,
I wish I could disappear.

Because even though I know:

I'm beautiful just the way I am.

What I look like doesn't matter.

It's what's on the inside that counts.

Since I love myself, it shouldn't matter what other people think...

I still have days where I don't feel good about my body.

Days when I don't love my body or myself.

You probably have days
like that too.

Everyone does.

And I'm going to tell you why.

ARE
REA

YOU DY?

What I'm about to tell you is kind of BIG.

IT'S

HU

GE
ACTUALLY.

GIGA

N   T   I   C.

There are a GAZILLION
companies and people
in the world who

claim they have products that will fix whatever is "wrong" with you.

They'll make your skin lighter.

They'll make your
muscles bigger.

They'll make your hair
straighter.

They'll make your teeth whiter.

They'll make you lose weight.

These companies would never make a single dollar if you didn't believe there was something about you that needed to be fixed.

So they spend LOTS OF MONEY
on advertisements to make you think
that if you buy their stuff,
you'll become
a little smaller,
a little prettier,
a little stronger,
and all of your problems will go away.

BUT THAT'S NOT TRUE.

Here's the real truth:

Nothing about you needs
to be fixed.

Your skin is the color it's supposed to be.

Your muscles are the size they're supposed to be.

Your hair is as curly as it's supposed to be.

Your teeth don't need to be any whiter than they already are.

And you don't need to lose weight.

Don't believe me?

Right now, your body is doing hundreds of things that let you think, feel, breathe, and live.

Your bones are growing, white blood cells are fighting off germs and viruses, your heart is pumping pints of blood all the way from your pinky toes to your pinky fingers.

Your body is amazing!

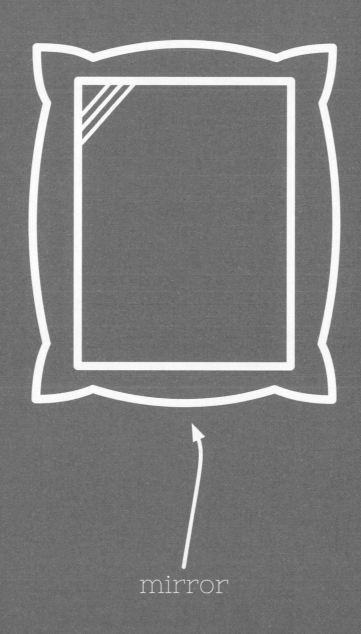

mirror

It is so good at stuff.

Scientists all over the world are trying to build robots and sensors and computers that do things as well as your body does them.

Your body is really freaking awesome.

And this very special body of yours, it can tell you what it needs.

Listen to it.

Let the voice that says,
"I'm hungry," speak louder
than the one that says,
"I have to be skinny."

Let the voice that says,
"That soccer game looks like fun,"
speak louder than the one that
says, "But what if I get sweaty?"

Let the voice that says,
"I really want to go swimming,"
speak louder than the one that
says, "But what if I look funny?"

Think about all the great things about you.

Maybe you're a really
fast runner.
Or you're a genius.
Or can eat a lot of
chicken nuggets.
Or maybe you're the best video
game player in your whole class.
You're a really good friend.
You always have the best ideas.
You're trustworthy.
You can turn any bad day
into a good one.

(If you can't think of anything that is great about you, ask a grownup—they'll know!)

All these things matter a lot.
They make you, you!

They're far more
important than
how your eyebrows look,
or whether
you have a pimple.

So repeat after me...

I am
who I am
who I am who
I am who I am who I am
who I am...

Get it?!
You are you.
Love your body.
It's yours and it's the
only one you'll ever have.

Outro

I'm so glad you stuck around to the end of this book. This is a tough subject and it probably brought up a lot of feelings. The most important thing for you to do right now is talk about those feelings.

Talk about them until you laugh. Talk about them until you cry. Talk about them until you finally say the thing you've been holding back.

And then keep talking about body image.

Meanwhile, surround yourself and the kids in your life with diverse forms of beauty. Follow models who look like you on social media. Watch TV and movies where people who look like you are the heroes. Read books that feature complicated, messy characters who remind you of yourself.

And if you can't find any of these things, I hope you make them.

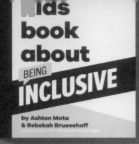

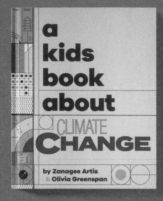
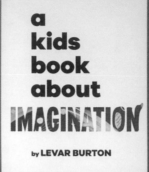
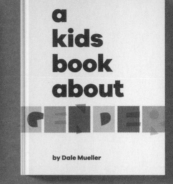

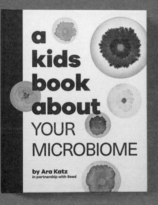
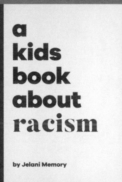

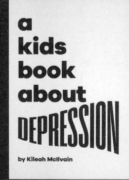